LEVEL 2 SCIENCE

LET'S READ AND FIND OUT

WHAT MAKES A BLIZZARD?

BY KATHLEEN WEIDNER ZOEHFELD

ILLUSTRATED BY MADDIE FROST

HARPER

An Imprint of HarperCollinsPublishers

Special thanks to Dr. Sonia Kreidenweis, Professor of Atmospheric Science at Colorado State University, for her valuable assistance.

The Let's-Read-and-Find-Out Science book series was originated by Dr. Franklyn M. Branley, Astronomer Emeritus and former Chairman of the American Museum of Natural History–Hayden Planetarium, and was formerly co-edited by him and Dr. Roma Gans, Professor Emeritus of Childhood Education, Teachers College, Columbia University. Text and illustrations for each of the books in the series are checked for accuracy by an expert in the relevant field. For more information about Let's-Read-and-Find-Out Science books, write to HarperCollins Children's Books, 195 Broadway, New York, NY 10007, or visit our website at www.letsreadandfindout.com.

For Geoff, who loves the snow—K.Z.

*For my brother, Brett, who made my childhood
memories of winter special*—M.F.

In the midwestern United States, it's always cold and snowy in winter. But the winter of 1887–88 was one of the coldest and snowiest the people there had ever seen. Most days, schools were closed because of the bad weather.

On January 12, 1888, everyone woke up to a sweet surprise. The morning sun gave off a warm, coppery glow. There was a mild breeze from the south, and the air felt as soft as velvet.

Children grabbed their books and walked to their one-room schoolhouses. The weather was so nice, they left their hats and mittens behind.

Parents hurried outdoors to catch up on farm chores or to hang quilts and blankets out to air. They hitched up their horses and wagons and went to nearby towns to shop.

Then, with no warning at all, a huge, rolling, blue-black bank of clouds appeared. It stretched across the whole northwestern horizon. A strange stillness fell over the land.

People stared in disbelief. What was it? They did not have to wait long for an answer. The dark clouds were moving toward them with astonishing speed.

11

The next minute, a blast of cold wind hit them—wind so strong it could knock a grown man over! The clouds blotted out the sun. The air became thick with powdery white snow. You couldn't see your own hands in front of your face.

Sharp snow needles blasted bare skin. Eyes and noses froze. It became almost impossible to breathe. Walking took every bit of strength you had.

Anyone caught out in the storm was in terrible danger. And lots of people were! Children trying to walk home from school became hopelessly lost. Farmers froze trying to get from their barns to their houses.

In the 1870s and 1880s, people first began using the word "**blizzard**" to describe winter storms like this one. Some say it came from the German word "blitz," meaning "bolt of lightning." Others say it's from the English word "blaze," used to describe something fast and violent, like a gunshot. Wherever it came from, the word stuck. Each terrible blizzard has become a part of our history. People tell stories of how they survived. And they tell the stories of those who didn't.

ATCHISON DAILY PA

ATCHISON, KANSAS, FRIDAY, JANUARY

SEIP & HORTON.
COMMERCIAL PRINTERS
&
OFFICE STATIONARY

THE CRUEL
BLIZZARD'

Coal Prices Busted.

THE POMEROY COAL COMPANY
SAYS SO!

READ THEIR PRICES:

Osage City

The Wichita Daily Eagle
Friday Morning, January 13, 1888.

HOWLING BLIZZARDS.

Several School Children Lost in
Huron, Dakota

All of Whom Have Been Found.

Railway Traffic Delayed
in the Northwest

WIN
FO

All Children's
Mittens

COLE &
The One-Price

New-York Tribu

NEW-YORK, FRIDAY, JANUARY 20,

ANOTHER STORM
IN DAKOTA

TRAINS AGAIN STOPPED
BY THE DRIFTS.

Historians named the blizzard of January 12, 1888, the "Schoolchildren's Blizzard." Not all blizzards are as violent as that one was. And not all snowstorms are blizzards, either. To be called a blizzard, a snowstorm must come with winds of 35 miles per hour (56 kilometers per hour) or more. And the strong wind has to last for at least three hours. There has to be enough snow in the wind to cause a **whiteout**. When weather reports talk about "whiteout conditions," they mean you can't see anything farther than one-quarter-mile away.

Blizzards can happen anyplace that has snow in winter. But the blizzards of the Midwest are among the worst in the world. And it's in the Midwest that it's easiest to see how and why blizzards form.

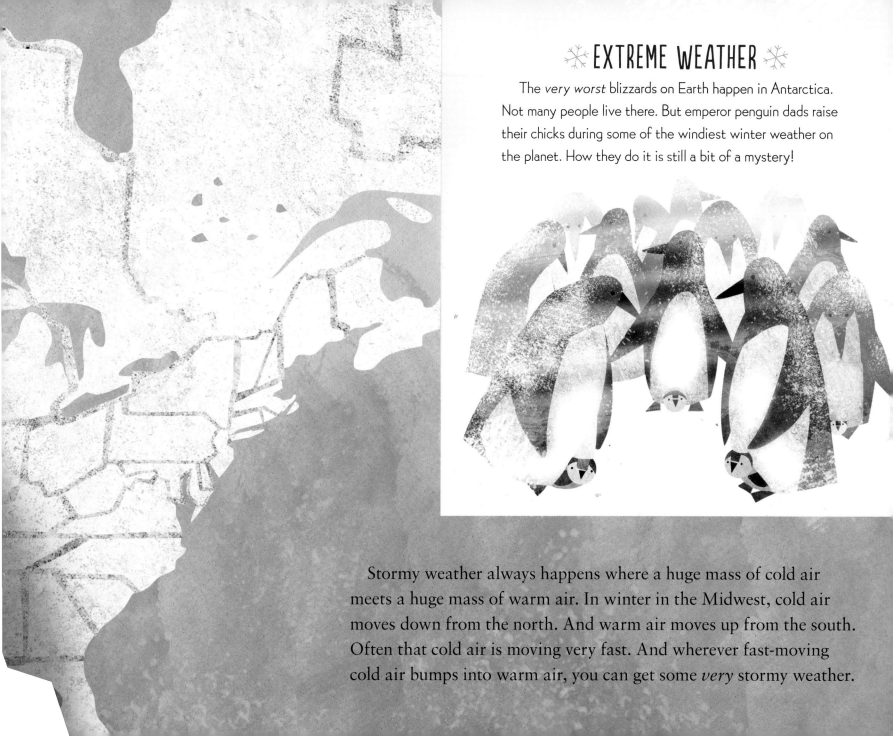

❄ EXTREME WEATHER ❄

The *very worst* blizzards on Earth happen in Antarctica. Not many people live there. But emperor penguin dads raise their chicks during some of the windiest winter weather on the planet. How they do it is still a bit of a mystery!

Stormy weather always happens where a huge mass of cold air meets a huge mass of warm air. In winter in the Midwest, cold air moves down from the north. And warm air moves up from the south. Often that cold air is moving very fast. And wherever fast-moving cold air bumps into warm air, you can get some *very* stormy weather.

Here's the reason why: Cold air is denser, and heavier, than warm air. The fast-moving cold air pushes under the warm air. The lighter warm air rises up and flows over the cold air.

One of the most important gases in air is **water vapor**. And warm air can hold a lot of it! Cold air can't hold as much water vapor as warm air.

COLD FRONT

Cold air

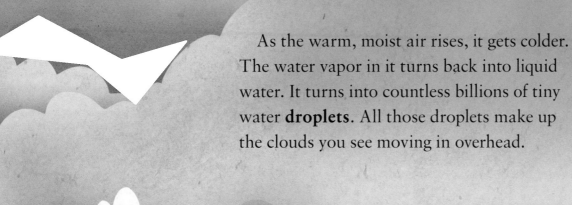

As the warm, moist air rises, it gets colder. The water vapor in it turns back into liquid water. It turns into countless billions of tiny water **droplets**. All those droplets make up the clouds you see moving in overhead.

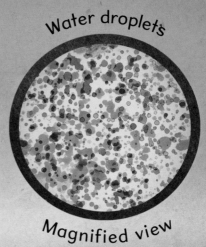

Water droplets

Magnified view

Warm air

❄ ABOUT FRONTS ❄

The area where a cold **air mass** meets a warm air mass is called a **front**.

In a warm front, a warm air mass pushes against a cold air mass. In a cold front, a cold air mass pushes against a warm air mass. Cold fronts always bring stormier weather than warm fronts.

All clouds are made up of water droplets that form when warm, moist air rises and cools. But if the air becomes very cold, some of the water vapor turns into tiny **ice crystals**.

More and more ice crystals form quickly. Soon there will be billions and billions of ice crystals and water droplets overhead. You see the storm clouds growing even bigger and darker.

Magnified view of ice crystals

❄ THE WATER CYCLE ❄

❉ Water vapor gets into the air through **evaporation.**
Evaporation is the process of changing from a liquid
(water) into a gas (water vapor).

❉ Water vapor turns back into liquid through **condensation.**
Condensation is the process of changing from a gas into
a liquid.

❉ The process of changing from a gas directly into a solid
(tiny ice crystals) is called **deposition.**

❉ Any liquid or solid water that falls to the Earth from clouds
is **precipitation.**

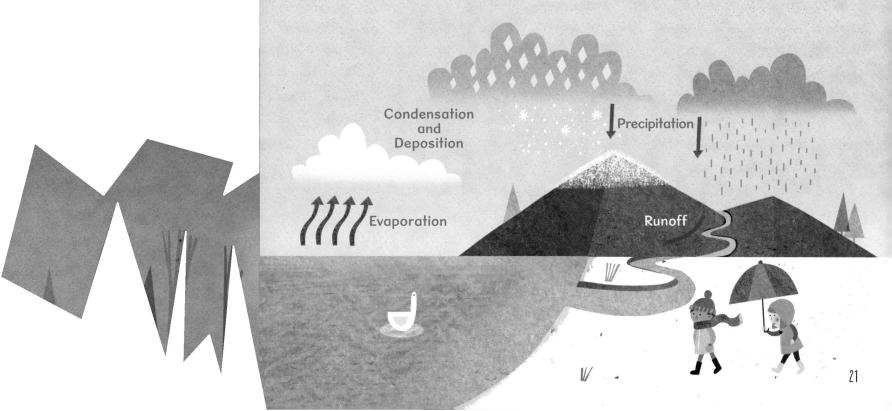

Condensation and Deposition

Precipitation

Evaporation

Runoff

In winter storm clouds, those tiny ice crystals gather more and more water vapor from the air. Once enough water vapor has frozen onto the ice crystals, they become snowflakes. When they are heavy enough, they begin to fall to the ground.

But a blizzard is much more than just falling snow!

❄ LOOKING AT SNOW ❄

Next time you are in a place where snow is falling, take a sheet of black paper and a magnifying glass outside. Catch some snow on the paper and have a close look. How many different snow shapes do you see?

Beautiful six-sided snowflakes are what most people think of when they think of snow. But sometimes snow takes on other shapes, such as flat, six-sided plates or even little six-sided columns. These columns can grow so long and thin, they look like tiny needles. When they are blown by a strong wind, snow needles can really sting!

When warm air rises, it creates a wide area of low pressure.
The people who woke to a nice warm morning on January
12, 1888, were in a low-pressure area. Low-pressure areas are
unstable. Fast-moving cold air blows in to fill the area where
the warm air is rising up.

People were stunned by how suddenly the wind blew in. And that wind was icy cold! In some areas, the **temperature** dropped by 40 degrees in a matter of minutes.

In a blizzard, falling snow is blown sideways by fast, freezing cold wind.

25

Even after the snow has stopped falling, blizzard winds can pick up snow from the ground and blow it around. This is called a ground blizzard. Blowing snow can pile up in drifts many feet high. In the Schoolchildren's Blizzard, snowdrifts completely buried many homes and schools. Once the blizzard had stopped, people had to dig tunnels just to get out their doors!

❄ ZOO ESCAPE ❄

In 1977, a blizzard hit Buffalo, New York. It left the city buried under snowdrifts for almost two weeks. At the Buffalo Zoo, the drifts were higher than many of the fences. The reindeer escaped by simply walking out of their pens.

Back in 1888, **meteorologists**—scientists who study weather—used many tools that we still use today. On January 12, they had figured out that a big winter storm was coming. But they did not have enough time to warn people so they could stay safe.

They used:

Thermometers to measure air temperature

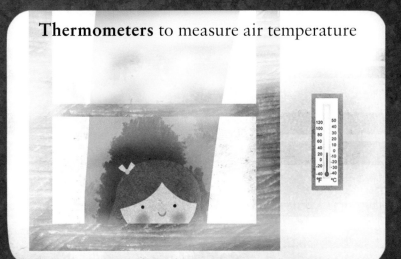

Barometers to measure **air pressure**

Pinwheel-like devices, called **anemometers**, to measure wind speed

Wind vanes to figure out the wind's direction

Over the years since then, scientists have invented new tools to help forecast the weather. Our high-tech tools help us figure out what the weather will be many days ahead of time.

Today we *also* have:

Radar stations that send out radio waves. The waves bounce off raindrops, snow, or other precipitation and return to the stations, like echoes. The waves tell meteorologists where a storm is, how big it is, and if there will be rain or snow.

Satellites in orbit around the Earth. Weather satellites send images of all the areas where clouds are forming. The images help meteorologists keep track of storm clouds as they move.

Supercomputers that help meteorologists process all the data and make predictions.

Unlike the people of 1888, you can get the latest weather report instantly on your TV or radio. Or you can check the weather app on your smartphone or computer. If dangerous weather is on the way, meteorologists at the U. S. National Weather Service will issue an alert.

A "blizzard watch" means there could soon be falling snow and strong winds in your area.

A "blizzard warning" means that high winds and blowing snow are expected or are already happening.

When a watch or warning is issued, it's time to get prepared! Driving is extremely dangerous during a blizzard. Warnings give people time to get food and supplies for their families before the storm hits. Heat and electricity may go out in a blizzard. It's good to have a flashlight and extra batteries on hand. If you have a fireplace or woodstove, it's good to have extra firewood, too.

Plan to stay indoors during a blizzard. If you must go outside, do not leave your hat and mittens behind! Wear warm boots and layers of clothing. Keep your face covered. And be aware that high winds can make cold temperatures feel much worse.

A really bad blizzard can last for several days. But eventually the wind will stop, and the sun will come out again. Snowplows will clear the streets. Sidewalks will be shoveled.

And then—it will be time for fun!

33

Keep a Winter Weather Journal for Your Area

You'll need:

❄ A small, blank notebook   ❄ An outdoor thermometer

❄ A pencil   ❄ A barometer (optional)

Monday, December 26

Temperature °F	Description
30 °F	cloudy and sunny

At the top of each notebook page, write the date and the day of the week. Your first date will be whatever day you decide to begin your journal. Plan to make your weather observations for a whole month. That way you will see how the weather in your area changes over a long period of time.

Divide each page into two sections, or three if you have a barometer at home or at school. Label the first section "Temperature." Plan to record the outdoor temperature at the same time, or times, each day. The second section will be for describing the weather (for example: Was the day sunny, cloudy, rainy, snowy?). If you have a barometer, you can add a third section for air pressure.

When you have finished your journal, you will have a lot of important data at your fingertips! If someone asks you what winter was like in your town, you can make a graph like this one to show them:

WEATHER GRAPH FOR DECEMBER

Number of days (y-axis: 1–14)

Categories: Sunny, Partly Cloudy, Cloudy, Rainy, Snowy, Blizzard!

GLOSSARY

Air mass: A huge body of air that is about the same temperature and holds about the same amount of water vapor throughout its whole volume. The movement of air masses causes changes in the weather.

Air pressure: The force or weight of the air pushing on a particular area. Air pressure can vary, but it averages about 14.7 pounds per square inch (1,013 millibars).

Anemometer: A tool used to measure wind speed. The most common type uses a set of spinning cups mounted on a shaft.

Barometer: A tool that measures air pressure. High, or rising, air pressure usually means fair weather. Low, or falling, pressure means rain or snow is on the way.

Blizzard: A violent winter storm with cold temperatures, strong winds, and lots of blowing snow.

Condensation: The process of changing from a gas into a liquid.

Deposition: The process of changing from a gas directly into a solid.

Droplet: A very tiny amount of water. One small-to-medium-size raindrop is made up of about one million droplets.

Evaporation: The process of changing from a liquid into a gas.

Front: The area where two different air masses meet.

Ice crystal: A very tiny bit of frozen, or solid, water.

Meteorologist: A scientist who studies the weather.

Precipitation: Any water, whether liquid or solid, that falls to the ground from clouds.

Radar: A system of instruments used to detect distant objects and to figure out how far away they are and how fast they are moving.

Satellite: Any object launched into orbit around the Earth.

Supercomputer: A very fast and powerful computer used for science and engineering.

Temperature: A measure of how warm or cold something is.

Thermometer: A tool for measuring heat. In weather reporting, a thermometer is used to measure the temperature of the air.

Water vapor: Water in the form of an invisible gas.

Whiteout: A weather hazard in which blowing snow makes it impossible to see very far in any direction.

Wind vane: A tool for telling the direction of the wind. Winds are always named for the direction from which they blow. So, a wind blowing from the northwest is called a northwest wind.

❄ WHAT MAKES A BLIZZARD? ❄

Snow

+

Wind

❄ Winds must be **35** mph or more.

❄ Strong winds must last for at least **3** hours.

+

Low visibility

❄ There must be so much snow that there's a whiteout.

=

A blizzard!

BE SURE TO LOOK FOR ALL OF THESE BOOKS IN THE LET'S-READ-AND-FIND-OUT SCIENCE SERIES: